How to Paint

by

Helen Webster

ARCTURUS

Arcturus Publishing Ltd
26/27 Bickels Yard
151–153 Bermondsey Street
London SE1 3HA

Published in association with

foulsham

W. Foulsham & Co. Ltd,
The Publishing House, Bennetts Close, Cippenham,
Slough, Berkshire SL1 5AP, England

ISBN 0-572-02884-9

British Library Cataloguing-in-Publication Data: a catalogue record for this
book is available from the British Library

Copyright ©2003 Arcturus Publishing Limited

Editor: Rebecca Panayiotou
Text design: Viki Ottewill
Cover design: Stünkel Studio

Printed in China

contents

introduction

How to Paint is an informative and fun introduction to the many different art mediums that are available to today's budding young artists. Watercolours, wax resistance, chalk pastels, collage, acrylic paints, tissue paper, oil paints, batik, the list goes on and on!

This book has been designed so that every double page spread serves as its own mini art class, each one an imaginative and exciting way to create a painting or picture using a different technique or medium. So to use this book, all you have to do is follow the simple step-by-step instructions and, before you know it, you'll have some amazing artistic masterpieces, and will have learnt a thing or two as well!

Before we get started then, let's have a quick look at some of the materials you'll be using:

wax crayons

watercolours

assorted paper and card

pot of water

paintbrushes

tissue paper

chalk pastels

poster paints

colouring pencils

felt tip pen and scissors

sticky tape and glue

acrylic paints

All of the different painting ideas in this book can be easily adapted, so whether you're using it as a learning guide, or whether you're already a competent artist dipping in for inspiration, have fun and be sure to experiment!

how to use colours

To create an effective painting it is useful to know about colours.

First of all, it's always helpful to learn about the primary colours. These are called primary because no other colours can be mixed together to make them. Yellow, red and blue are the building blocks of most paintings.

You can have lots of fun mixing primary colours together. When you do this, the resulting colour is called a secondary colour.

when you mix the primary colours together you make secondary colours

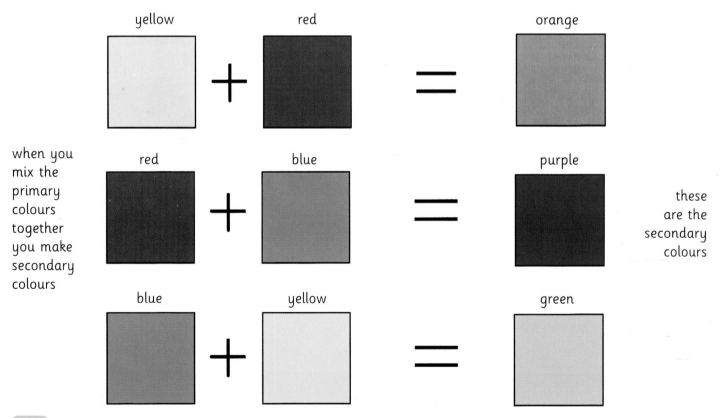

these are the secondary colours

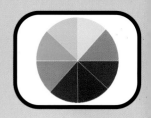

When painting, you might sometimes want to refer to something called a 'colour wheel'. A colour wheel firstly helps us to see what colours are complementary (these are the ones sitting opposite each other on the wheel) and secondly, it highlights harmonious colours. (These are the ones that are lying next to each other on the wheel.)

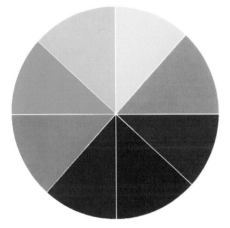

the colours that sit directly opposite each other on the colour wheel are called the complementary colours. This is because they contrast beautifully when put together

these are the complementary colours

Another thing to take into account when painting is the tone. This can make the difference between a vivid strong picture and a subtle pale picture. Changing the tone can change the whole atmosphere of the picture.

light → → → → → dark

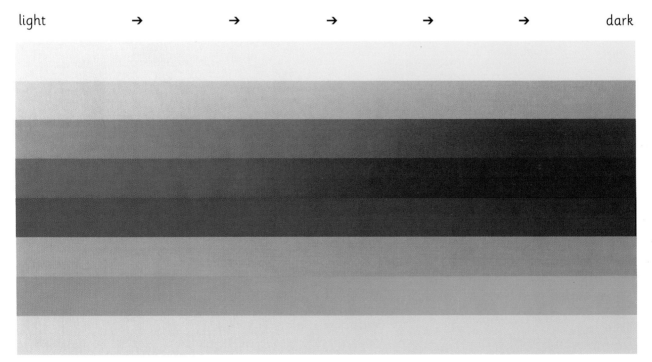

the tone of a colour is determined by how light or dark it is. You can change the tone by adding white to your paint or by making the paint more runny with water. (If you are using oil paints you will need to add oil paint thinner instead of water.)

how to use harmonious colours

We are now going to investigate the different effects we can create by mixing the primary colours.

When painting in shades of colour made up from yellow and red, you find that the picture has an overall effect of looking strong and bright.

yellow ➔ red

When painting in shades of colour made up from red and blue, you will find that the picture has an overall effect of looking warm and rich.

red ➔ blue

When painting in shades of colour made up from blue and yellow, you will find that the picture has an overall effect of looking cool and fresh.

blue ➔ yellow

When you experiment mixing all three primary colours, you get a rainbow of colours, which gives you more choice and a never-ending range of effects.

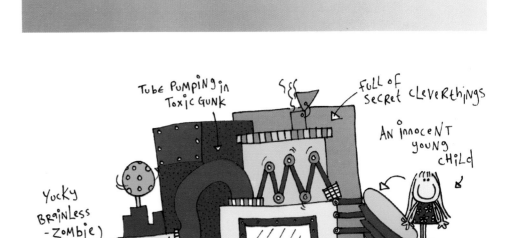

mixture of all 3 primary colours

Which painting do *you* prefer?

how to use shadows and shading

When painting anything, it's very handy to know about different shades and where to put shadows. First of all you have to think about where the light is coming from.

The rule about shading is that the further away an object is from the light source, the darker the shade should be.

As for shadows, where we put them in our painting will depend on the direction of the light, as can be seen on the opposite page.

light source

notice how the brown shade gets darker the further away the floor is from the light source. The same applies to the wall and the bowl

have a really dark shadow underneath anything that touches the floor

try to make the shadow vaguely echo the shape of its figure

Look at this picture to see how different light sources create different shadows.

light C would create shadow...

light B would create shadow...

light D would create shadow...

light A would create shadow...

light E would create shadow...

shadow E

shadow A

shadow D

shadow B

shadow C

So if the light was coming from here, where would the shadow be?

Would the tail be a lighter shade of orange than the head?

Where would the darkest shades be?

how to create a snow scene using chalk pastels

you will need:

some chalk pastels

a piece of dark coloured paper

Let's draw a snow scene!

the direction of the light source

where the darkest shadows will be

Get your dark piece of paper and, using a light brown pastel, lightly sketch in the reindeer shape.

Use a white pastel to draw a faint circle in the top right-hand corner, to remind us where the light is coming from. Then draw the basic shape of the snowman.

Now we have to decide which colours to use for the different shadows. I am going to use yellow, light brown, dark brown and purple for the reindeer, and white, blue and purple for the snowman.

So let's begin building up the image.

Start with the highlights: the light brown and white.

Then move on to the shadows: the purple.

Fill in the main body of the reindeer.

Go over the highlighted areas again, and then do the same with the shadows, so that there is a greater contrast.

Finally, get a white pastel and create the falling snow with lots of dots and smudges.

how to paint in perspective using watercolours

you will need:

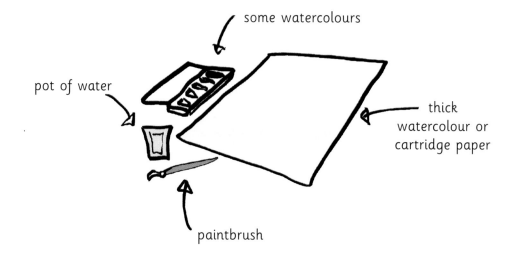

some watercolours

pot of water

paintbrush

thick watercolour or cartridge paper

Whenever you paint a picture that has a foreground and background, always remember that the stronger colours are at the front, and the lighter ones are at the back.

This landscape is a perfect example. Start with the furthest away subject first – in this case it's the sky. Paint this in with a pale pinky purple.

always sketch the picture in pencil first

Paint the mountains in blue. As they get nearer you should use darker and darker blue.

wet each section before you paint on it

Keep going!

if it's not dark enough, go over it again

The closest mountain and the castle should be the strongest blue and will have the most detail.

There you go! You now know how to paint in perspective!

how to paint a flower
using mixed watercolours

you will need:

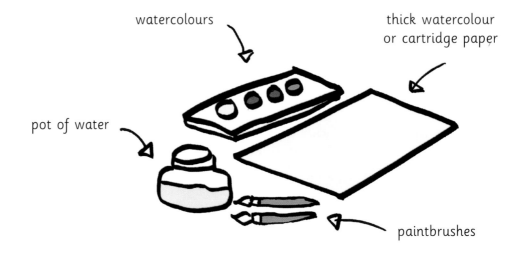

watercolours

thick watercolour
or cartridge paper

pot of water

paintbrushes

The fantastic thing about watercolours is the way that you can make so many wonderful shades just by mixing a few colours. As you can see with the painting of the flower, you can produce loads of different hues when you apply wet colour on to more wet colour.

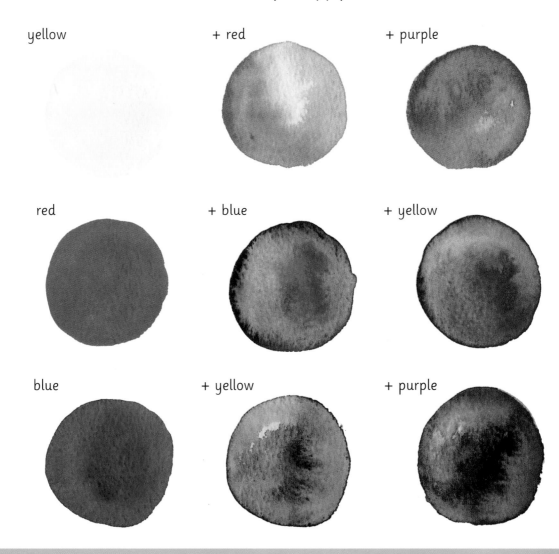

yellow	+ red	+ purple
red	+ blue	+ yellow
blue	+ yellow	+ purple

Simply decide on your base colour (I've used yellow here) and paint it on to your page, making sure that it is quite watery. Immediately add another colour to your wet paint, and then another, and so on. The effect is a kaleidoscope of colours and shades.

This technique is very handy when you want to paint something that has a large tonal range.

you need to leave gaps when applying wet colour on to wet colour. Otherwise all the colours would run across the whole petal

the centre of the flower is yellow plus red plus purple

the base shade is yellow. Then add light red

start off with yellow. Then add blue and green

again, start off with yellow. Then add orange and brown

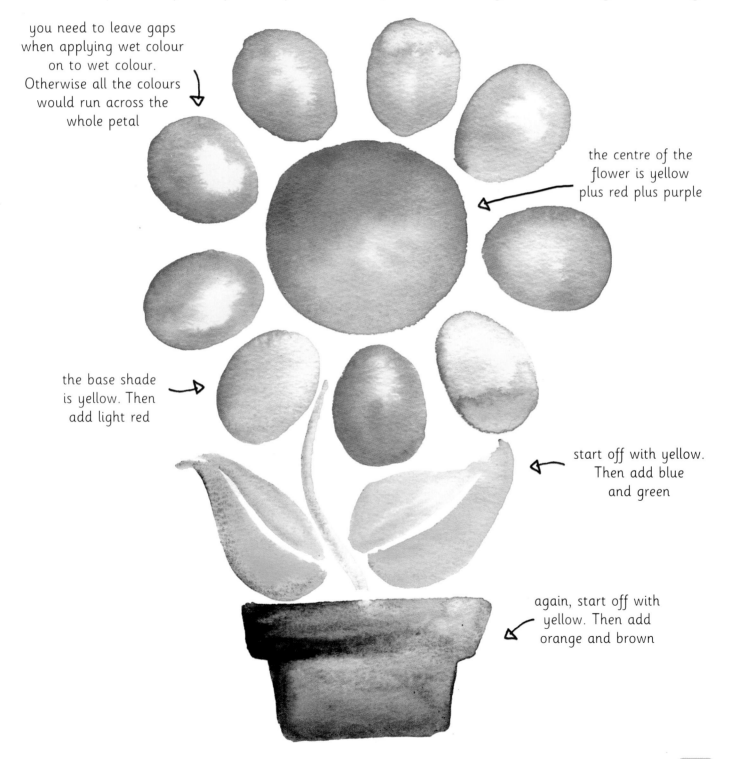

how to paint the loch ness monster using watercolours

you will need:

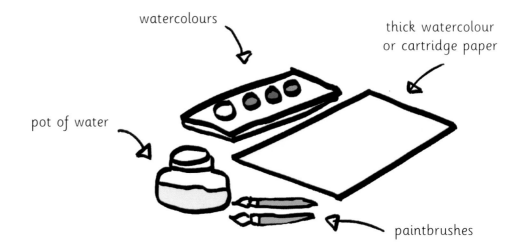

watercolours

thick watercolour or cartridge paper

pot of water

paintbrushes

Let's start with the lake. First wet the area that you want to paint before going over it again with the blue colour. This way you can easily add different shades of blue to the lake, giving it depth.

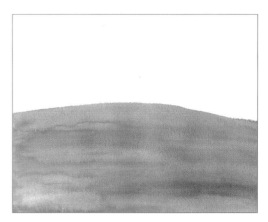

To paint the sky, do the same thing: wet the area first and then go over it with watercolour. Leave a zig-zag space for the mountains. To make really good cloud shapes, get a tissue, scrunch it up in your hand, and dab at the wet blue sky.

Now get your green paint and fill in the mountains. Remember that the further away they are, the lighter the green you should use.

Making sure that the lake is bone dry, get your paintbrush and dip it into some strong yellowy-white paint. Don't add too much water, as you want the paint to be really thick. Now paint in three arcs, a long wiggly neck and a head.

When that has dried, add a tiny bit of brown to the watercolour mixture and go over the monster again.

Finally, get a thin paintbrush, mix up a strong brown colour, and go around the outline of your Loch Ness monster. Then add his mouth and eyes. You might even like to paint on some scales – this is done by painting lots of little 'u's on his body.

how to paint a mermaid place mat using watercolours

you will need:

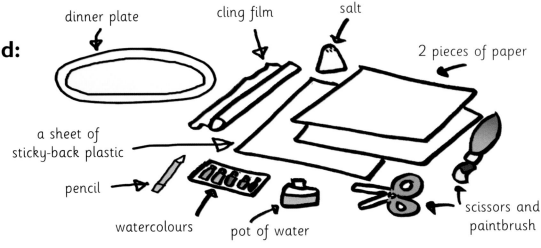

dinner plate

cling film

salt

2 pieces of paper

a sheet of sticky-back plastic

pencil

watercolours

pot of water

scissors and paintbrush

First draw the basic shape of your mermaid faintly in pencil. This will be a handy guide for when you paint.

When the paint and salt have completely dried, brush the salt off. You are left with a really cool effect – the tail looks as if it has scales!

Next start filling in the skin with a pale nude colour.

Get some brown and paint in the hair. Then use some red for the bikini top.

Paint the whole tail with yellow. Then, while it's still wet, add some red and orange to it. Finally, get some salt and sprinkle it over the tail.

Wait until it has all dried and cut the mermaid out.

Now get your other piece of paper and wet it with your brush before painting it blue. Get some cling film from the kitchen and put it over the wet piece of paper.

Keep it there until the paint has dried. When you take the cling film off, you will see that it has left a wicked watery pattern!

Get a dinner plate, put it on your blue page, and draw round it. Now remove the plate and use the drawn circle as a guide to cut out the shape of your place mat.

Put the mermaid on the blue circle. Place a sheet of sticky-back plastic over the top, cut round the edges and, hooray, you have yourself a mermaid place mat!

how to paint a water scene using wax resistance

you will need:

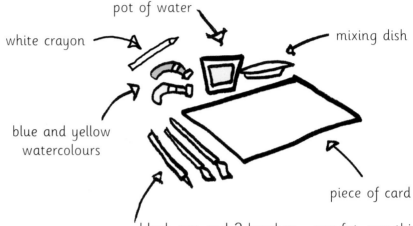

pot of water

white crayon

mixing dish

blue and yellow watercolours

piece of card

black pen and 2 brushes – one fat, one thin

Decide on your image (be it a fish, an octopus, or whatever) and draw it out using a black pen.

Then get a white crayon and carefully draw in the detail.

Now get your blue watercolour. Mix it with a lot of water and paint over the whole page with your big paintbrush.

Now, using the smaller paintbrush, mix the blue again but this time use a very small amount of water. Carefully go over your black pen lines.

Still using the blue, paint in extra details like more scales and emphasize the plants.

Finally, mix the yellow watercolour with some water (but don't make it too runny), and paint over the fish to make it stand out.

Finito!

how to do a scratch resistance painting using primary colours

you will need:

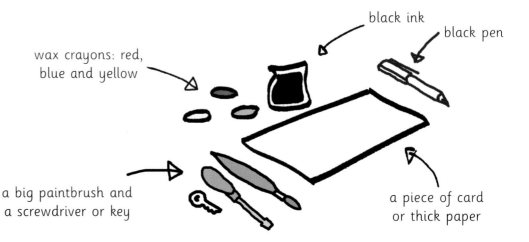

black ink

black pen

wax crayons: red, blue and yellow

a big paintbrush and a screwdriver or key

a piece of card or thick paper

First of all, draw out your name in block capitals. Make sure that all the letters are quite close to each other.

Now go round the outline of your name with a black pen, so that it is turned into one big shape.

Get your red and blue wax crayons and colour in the letters.

Finish off with a yellow crayoned background.

Now get your black ink and, using a big brush, paint over the whole image.

Wait until the ink has dried. Then, using a screwdriver or a key, scrape enough ink away to reveal the coloured wax underneath.

Have fun making different patterns and shapes in the remaining ink.

how to paint a cat using batik

you will need:

an iron

a thin piece of paper and some old newspaper

wax crayons

big paintbrush

red poster paint

black pen

As before, draw out your image in thick black pen first.

Get your wax crayons and colour in the picture. (You can't tell, but I have used white crayon in the white areas: this is a good colour to use as it stands out really well.)

Carefully scrunch the picture into a ball. Try not to rip it!

Un-scrunch it, get your red poster paint and cover the whole picture with it. Wait until this is completely dry.

Ask an adult to help you with the next step.

Switch the iron on, turning it to the cool setting. While it's heating up, get two sheets of old newspaper and put the painting in between them. Now iron the newspaper with your crumpled painting inside.

Finished! I really like the textured effect you get. It looks all crumpled, multi-coloured and cool.

how to paint an exotic bird using collage

you will need:

acrylics or poster paints

pot of water

paintbrush

black felt tip pen

a piece of paper and an A4 piece of card

glue stick

Get a piece of paper and paint lots of different colours on it. Make sure you include quite a few shades of green!

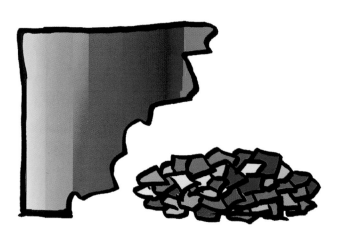

Wait until it dries. Then rip the paper into little pieces. Sort the colours into different piles.

Take all the bits of paper from your green pile and start to stick them on to a thick piece of A4 paper or card.

Continue until the whole page is covered. If you run out of green pieces just paint some more or rip up a picture of some green foliage from a magazine or newspaper.

When the glue has dried, get a thick black pen and roughly draw out the shape of your bird.

Use your yellow pieces of paper to make the beak. Use blue, orange and red pieces for the bird's body. Have fun using whatever colours you want for the tail feathers.

Finally, go over the outline of the bird again with your marker pen to complete the picture.

how to build a space rocket using paper collage

you will need:

black card and coloured paper

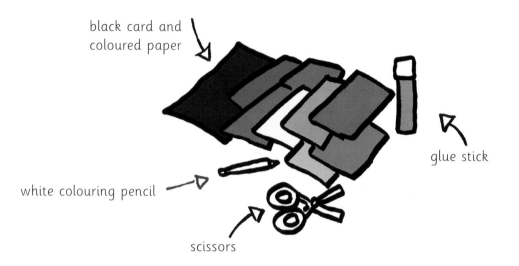

glue stick

white colouring pencil

scissors

First of all, take your white colouring pencil and cover the black card with lots of little stars.

Then, using different coloured paper for each shape, cut out a rectangle, a triangle, and something that looks like a piece of toast! These are the main body of your rocket.

Now start to add on extra shapes to build up the image.

To make flames, draw these three shapes on to red, orange and yellow paper. Each one should be smaller than the one before. Cut them out and place them on top of each other to give the appearance of flames.

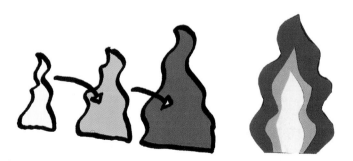

To make the moon, cut out one big circle and one squished circle. Then cut out the middle of the squished circle to make a ring. Carefully slot the full circle into the ring and hey presto you have yourself a moon!

Your space rocket should now be looking something like this.

Now, using thin strips and circles of coloured paper, build up the detail on the rocket and the moon.

You can have fun making other pictures as well…

how to make a sunflower scene using tissue paper

you will need:

a pencil

a piece of paper and lots of tissue paper

glue stick

black ball-point or felt tip pen

First of all, sketch out the picture lightly in pencil.

Now get the yellow tissue paper and rip out the rough shapes of the heads of the sunflowers. Stick these down with glue.

Get the blue tissue paper and stick it down around the top edges.

Stick some green tissue paper in the bottom half of the picture. Now the whole page is filled with colour!

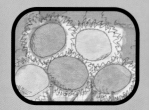

This is when you start to layer the colours. Add more orange and yellow to the centres of the sunflowers.

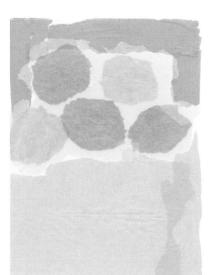

Now it's time to add the foliage. Rip up thin strips of green and stick them down.

Lastly, get your black pen and add any details and outlines that you want.

how to paint a boat using only tissue paper!

you will need:

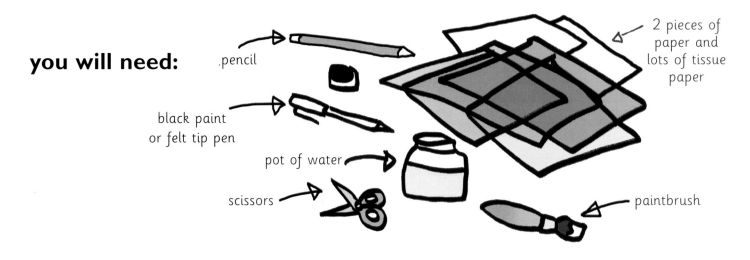

pencil

black paint or felt tip pen

pot of water

scissors

2 pieces of paper and lots of tissue paper

paintbrush

I bet you didn't think that you could paint with tissue paper, did you? Well you can, and this is how:

First of all, get a piece of paper and draw a rough outline of what you are going to paint. This will act as a useful guide.

Then cut out a big rectangle of blue tissue paper. This will be the background colour. Place it on a new piece of paper.

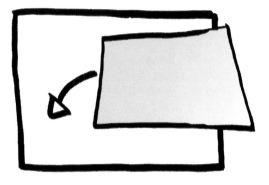

Get a paintbrush, wet it, and brush the water over the tissue paper, making sure that it is completely covered.

Now carefully pull the tissue paper off. There will be a blue rectangular print of colour left on the page! Wow!

Now do the same with the boat. Get some brown tissue paper, cut out the shape and position it on your piece of paper. Wet the tissue paper using your paintbrush again. Then peel off.

Do exactly the same thing with the sails (which are just two triangles).

Then do the sun (a yellow circle) and the anchor.

Finally, get a felt tip or some black paint and outline the edges. This helps to make the picture look stronger, but you don't have to do it if you don't want to.

how to make greetings cards

you will need:

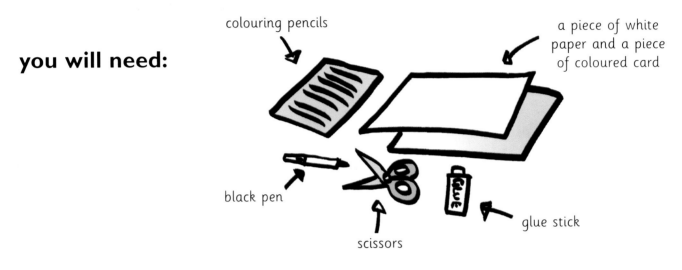

colouring pencils

a piece of white paper and a piece of coloured card

black pen

scissors

glue stick

This is a really easy, yet impressive way to make cards for your family and friends!

Get your plain piece of paper and draw four small boxes in black ball-point or felt tip. Inside the boxes draw pictures that are suitable for the occasion. For example, I'm making a greetings card for my niece's first birthday, so I have drawn a pram, some building blocks, a cake and a rocking horse.

Now get your colouring pencils and colour in the black and white drawings. Get some scissors and cut out the square with your four pictures inside.

Now pick up your piece of coloured card and carefully fold it in half. Position it so that it opens up on the right-hand side.

Stick your square of pictures on to the front of the coloured card with some glue or double-sided sticky tape.

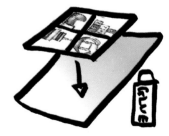

Finally, get a piece of paper, write the message that you want to say (I've put, 'Happy 1st Birthday' on mine), colour it in, cut it out, and stick it at the top of your card.

Hey presto! Easy quick cards that look great!

Here are some more cards that I have made:

how to paint a monster using acrylics

you will need:

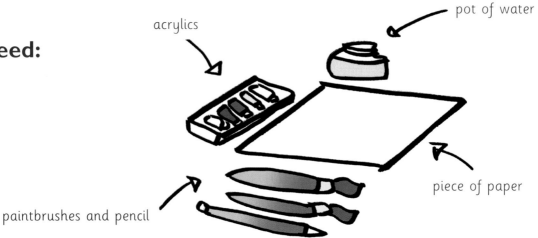

acrylics

pot of water

piece of paper

paintbrushes and pencil

The wonderful thing about acrylic paint is that you can have fun making marks in the paint while it's still wet. Also, because it's so thick, it's really easy to add lots of colours on top of each other without ending up with a smudgy mess!

I'm going to use acrylics to paint a monster. The first thing to do is to paint its body. Apply the blue acrylic really thickly. Then, while it's still wet, use the end of the brush to make little lines in the paint. These will be white because the paper underneath is showing through.

Next, paint the arms, legs, eyes and mouth in bright yellow. This will be easier if you draw them out lightly in pencil first.

Now fill in the background with red.

Wait until it is dry. Get some white paint and cover the background in white spots. Acrylic is the only paint that lets you do this – that's why it's so much fun! You can add as many colours on top of each other as you want, without worrying that the colours are going to smudge or go muddy.

Finally, use dark brown to finish off the eyes, and add any last-minute details that you want (like the blue on the white spots).

how to spot paint using acrylics

you will need:

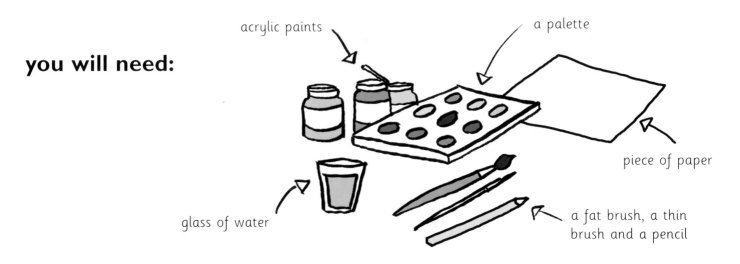

acrylic paints

a palette

piece of paper

glass of water

a fat brush, a thin brush and a pencil

Draw out your tortoise and, using your big paintbrush, fill the page with strong colours.

Now take your smaller paintbrush and dip it into a bright yellow paint. Very lightly spot the colour around the shape of the tortoise.

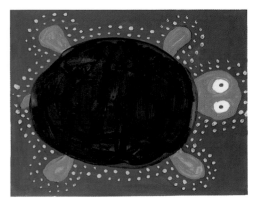

Your picture should now look like this.

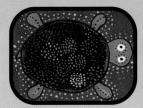

Once you have gone round the tortoise a few times, change the colour of the spots to orange or red. Continue to do this until the whole background is covered.

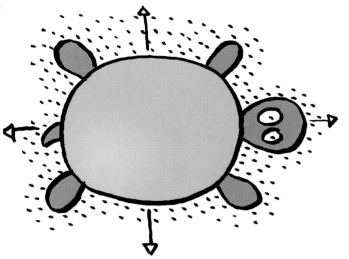

Now move on to the shell. Paint your spots in a winding circular pattern, so that they look like mini whirlpools. Do lots and lots of these different coloured whirlpools until the shell is full.

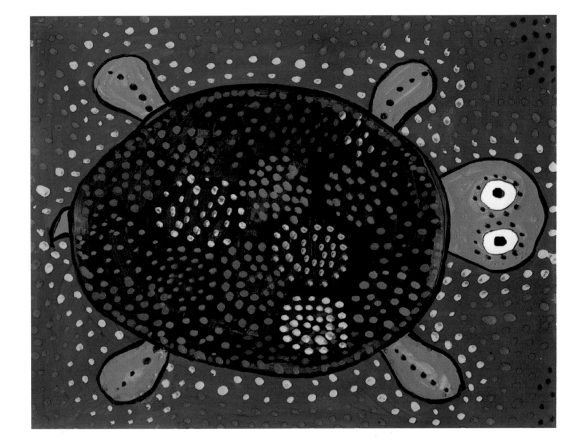

Finally, add extra spots to any other places that might need them.

how to paint a near and far landscape using oil paints

you will need:

oil paints

3 pieces of paper

oil paint thinner

pencil

scissors

glue

paintbrushes

Now we are going to learn about painting near and far. To do this we are going to paint a landscape. Get your three pieces of paper. On the first piece, paint the sky and far away hills. This should not contain much detail.

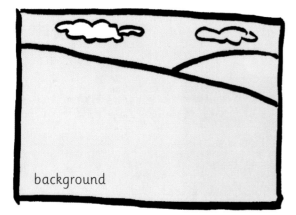

background

On the second piece, paint closer, smaller hills with a few trees on them. This should have a bit more detail. When the painting is dry, cut it out.

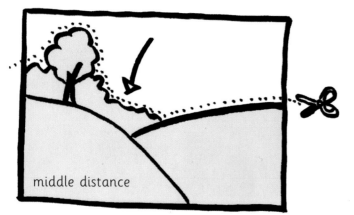

middle distance

On the third and final piece, paint a close up of a hill with an animal or some flowers on it. I have added some sheep. This sheet should contain the biggest, most detailed images. Again, when it is dry, cut it out.

foreground

Now place your two cut-outs on to your background. Immediately the painting has depth and perspective. It's a tricky technique made simple!

placing the 3 layers together creates depth

not much detail in the background

add different colour and texture to each hill

you have the closest image at the front of the picture

how to create a picture using colouring pencils

you will need:

lots of colouring pencils   a piece of paper

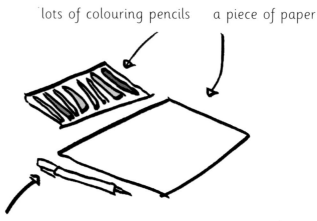

felt tip pen or pencil

I think colouring pencils are brilliant. You can use them in lots of different ways and they're really good for layering colour upon colour – just like I've done here with the cat!

First of all, let's have a look at a few colouring techniques you might want to use in your artwork:

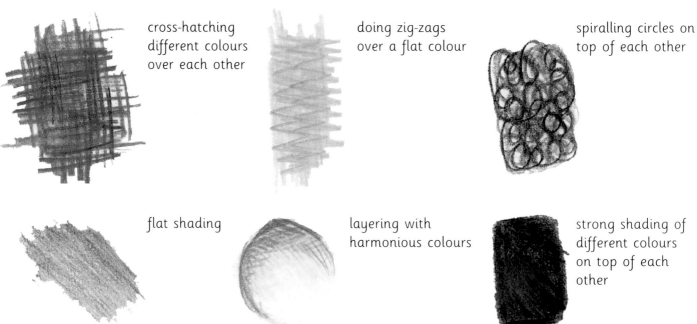

cross-hatching different colours over each other

doing zig-zags over a flat colour

spiralling circles on top of each other

flat shading

layering with harmonious colours

strong shading of different colours on top of each other

Great! Now let's put them into practice in a picture.

As usual, it's handy to draw out the image in pen or pencil first. It helps you to remember what and where to colour in.

Now colour in all of the picture, quickly and lightly. You want as much of the page covered as possible. This is so that you know roughly where the different colours are going to go.

Now start on the biggest and most complicated part of the picture – in this case it's the roof. Once you get to this stage, you can start to use the different colouring techniques we've just looked at. For the roof, I am going to use strong shades of different colours on top of each other. This creates depth.

Once the roof is done, colour each item in the picture one by one: first the wood, then the grass and sprawling plant, then the pathway, and finally the sky.

The rich blue sky was achieved by cross-hatching. It's a really easy thing to do and immediately adds texture to a picture.

how to make a city scene using black paper and colouring pencils

you will need:

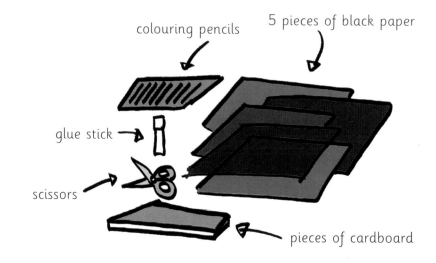

colouring pencils

5 pieces of black paper

glue stick

scissors

pieces of cardboard

I love colouring pencils because they work just as well on dark paper as they do on light. To illustrate this, let's create a bustling city by night.

Okay. Get your five pieces of paper. On the first one, you simply draw a moon at the top. Put this piece of paper to one side. Later we will stick the other layers on to this.

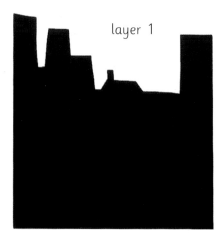

layer 1

On your second piece of paper, draw a city skyline reaching about two-thirds of the way up. Cut round the skyline and then draw the vague outline of the buildings with a white pencil. Then add some quick shading with yellow and orange.

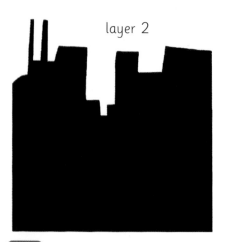

layer 2

On the next piece of paper, draw a city horizon – a little shorter than the last layer. Cut it out. Then add the building's features in white. Finish off the features in whatever colours you want.

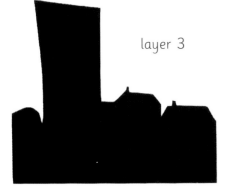

layer 3

Follow the same procedure with the next piece of paper, but this time the skyline should be shorter again. Remember that the closer the buildings are, the more detail and colour they have.

layer 4

Now draw Layer 4. This has the most detail and is the shortest skyline.

When you are happy with all four layers, you will be ready to stick them, one at a time, on to the first piece of paper which you have put to one side. Or, if you want to give the image more depth, you can stick each layer on to a piece of cardboard first. Then, when they are placed on top of each other, the depth will be exaggerated to create more of a 3-D look.